poems and paintings by

Douglas Florian

harcourt, inc.
San Diego · New York · London

bow wow meow meow

it's rhyming cats and dogs

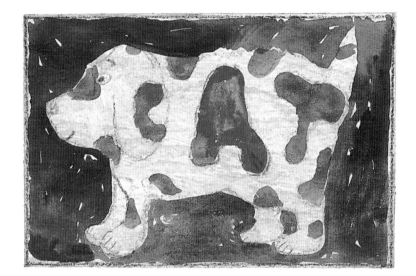

www.HarcourtBooks.com

Library of Congress Cataloging-in-Publication Data
Florian, Douglas.
Bow wow meow meow: it's rhyming cats and dogs/Douglas Florian.
p.   cm.
Contents: Dog log—The Chihuahua—The bloodhound—The bulldog—
The poodles—The pointers—The sheepdog—The Dalmatian—
The whippet—The wolf—The dachshund—
Cat chat—The Persian—The cheetah—The ocelots—The Siamese—
The lion—The Manx—The leopard—The jaguarundi—
The black panther.
1. Cats—Juvenile poetry.   2. Dogs—Juvenile poetry.
3. Children's poetry, American.
[1. Cats—Poetry.   2. Dogs—Poetry.   3. American poetry.]   I. Title
PS3556.L589B69   2003
811'.54—dc21   2002006309
ISBN 0-15-216395-6

C E G H F D B

MANUFACTURED IN CHINA

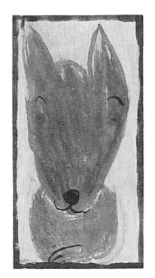

On
Blessed Memory
of
Alex Bloom

Contents

Dog Log

Rolled out of bed.
Scratched my head.
Brought the mail.
Wagged my tail.
Fetched a stick.
Learned a trick.
Chased a hare.
Sat in a chair.
Chewed a shoe—
Table, too.
Got in a spat
With a cat.
Buried a bone.
Answered the phone.
Heard a thief.
Gave him grief.
Time to creep
Off to sleep.

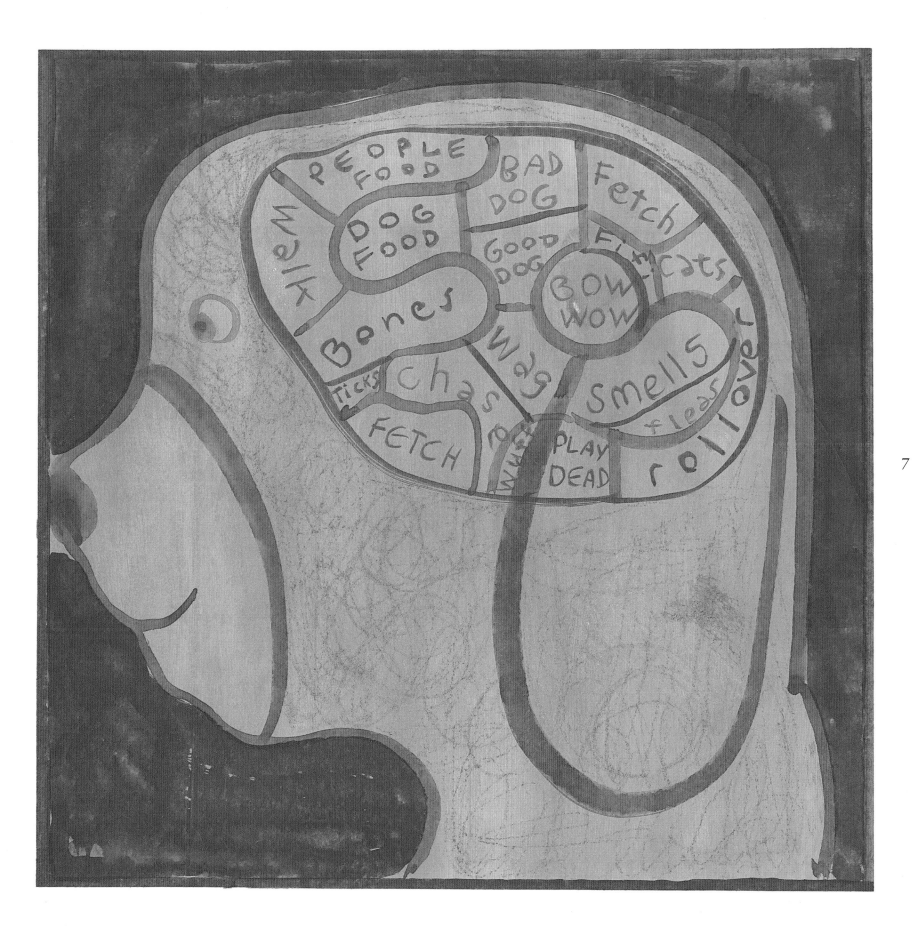

The Chihuahua

Chihuahua seems a sorry sight:
So small in stature, weight, and height.
But it can bark a brouhaha:
¡Chi-hua! ¡hua! ¡hua! ¡hua! ¡hua! ¡hua! ¡hua!

The Bloodhound

My big nose knows
Where my prey goes.
Fresh tracks I track
On ground or snows.
My stride is wide.
My ears are full.
My senses are
Scent-sational.

10

The Bulldog

The bulldog's face is full of pride.
His eyes look wise.
His jaw is wide.
His chin is straight.
His nose is strong.
His brow is great.
His jowls are long.
I'd say his face was full of charm
If he would let go of my arm.

The Poodles

Poodles have oodles and oodles of curls.

Which makes poodle boys look like poodle girls.

The curls may have whirls, while the whirls may have swirls.

Poodles have oodles and oodles of curls.

The Pointers

Some pointers point at foxes.
Some pointers point at hares.
Some pointers point at pheasants.
Mine points at Frigidaires.

The Sheepdog

The sheepdog is shaggy,
As shaggy as sheep.
It's shaggy as shaggy can be.
And over its face, all its shaggy hairs creep.
I wonder how sheepdogs can see.

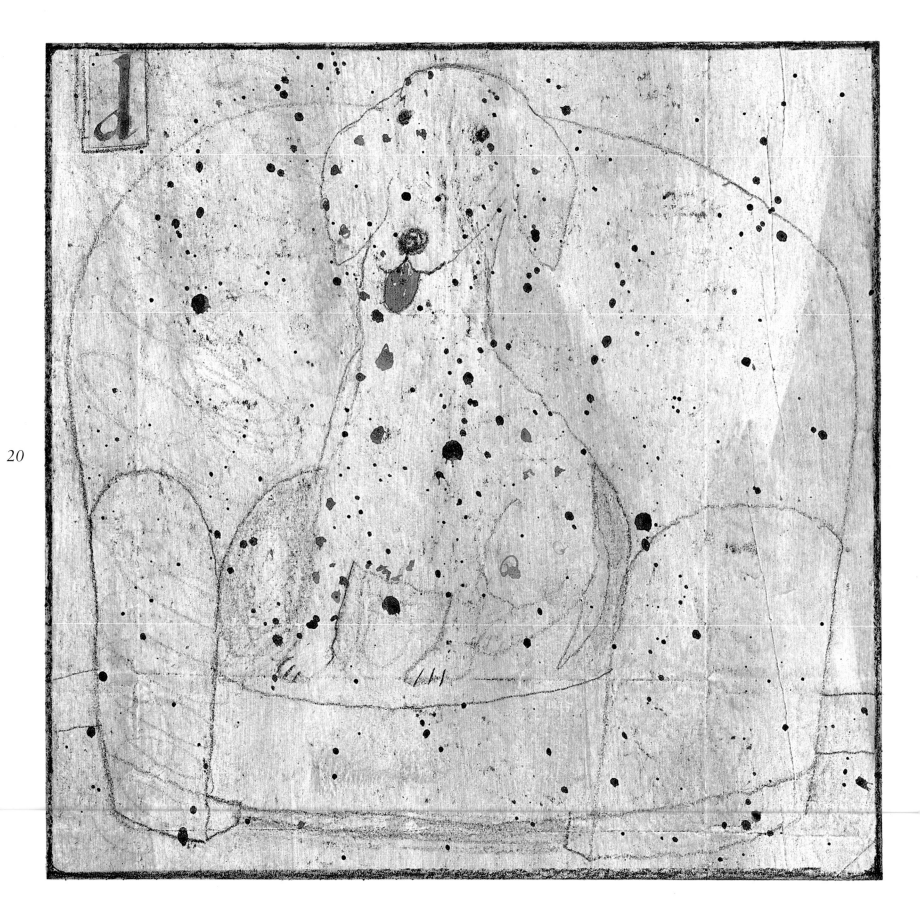

The Dalmatian

●f sp●ts y●u've g●t
An awful l●t.
M●re ●ften than n●t,
Y●u're easy t● sp●t.

The Whippet

The whippet speeds with ease and grace.
Few dogs can *whippet* in a race.
And it would make a wondrous pet,
Although *I* haven't caught one yet.

24

The Wolf

The wolf is cousin to the dog—
Except the wolf eats like a hog.
It doesn't use a bowl or dishes
But chews in any place it wishes.
Its table manners are quite rude:
The wolf will wolf down all its food.
And though a dog eats from a pan,
The wolf must feed catch-as-catch-can.

The Dachshund

Short up front
And short behind
But so long in-between.
The fleas all ride
Upon my side
In my s t r e t c h limousine.

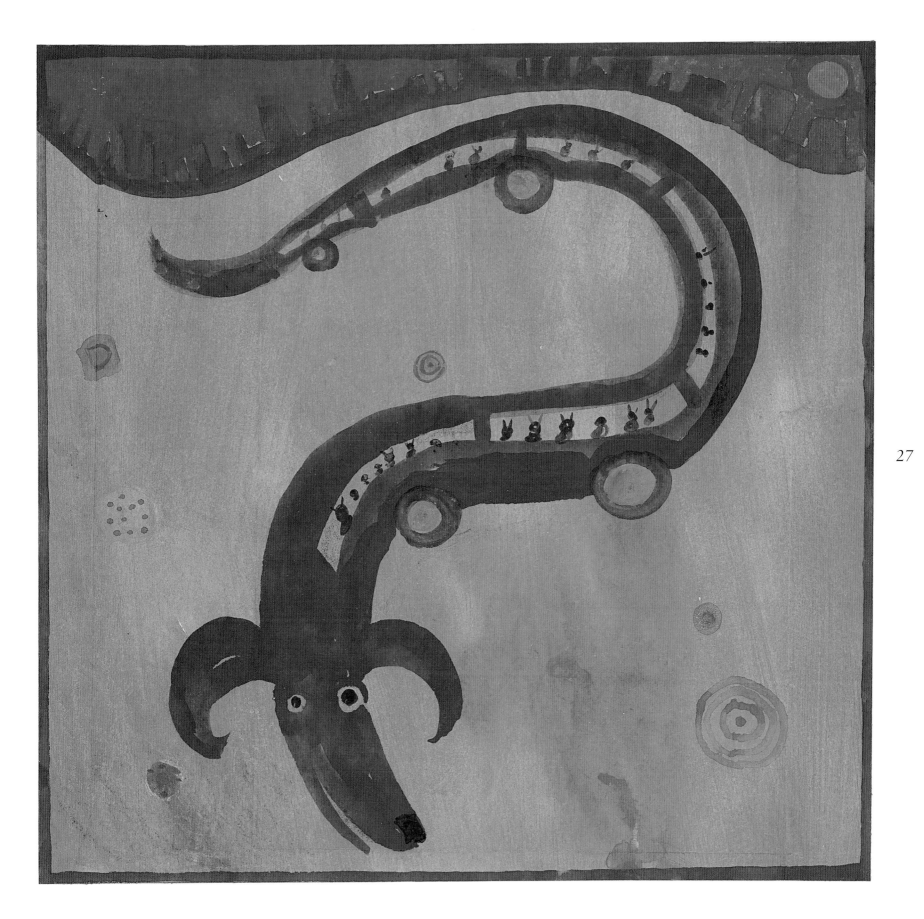

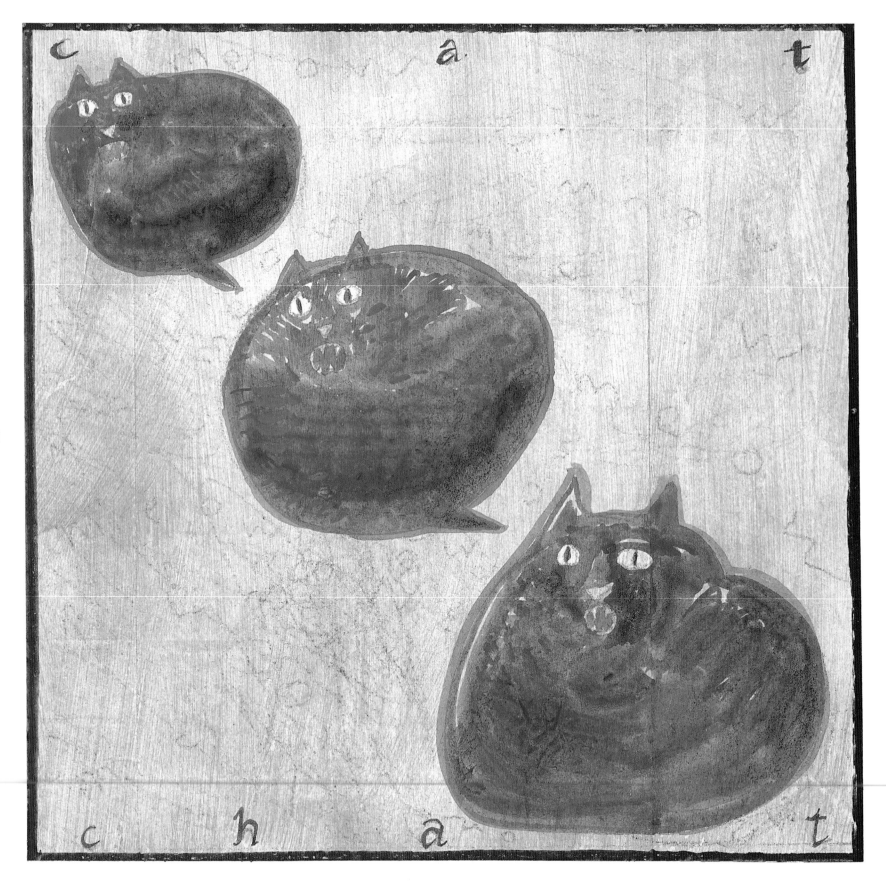

Cat Chat

You have sharp claws
But velvet paws.
You chase down rats.
Race other cats.
You nap all day.
Then wake to play
With balls of string.
All night you sing.
You make a fuss.
You're cur-i-ous.
You have soft fur
And love to purr.
You steal my chair
Then stare at air.
You are a cat
And that is that.

Scat!

The Persian

I am a cat of longhaired version.
A pet-igree that's known as purrrsian.

The Cheetah

The cheetah is *fleet*.
The cheetah is *fast*.
Its four furry feet
Have already passed.

The Ocelot

34

Why ocelots have lots of spots puzzles Ocelot.

The Siamese

I am a cat.
A cat I am.
My ancestors
Were from Siam.
My ears are brown.
My eyes are blue.
And **I'm** the boss, you know,
Not **you!**

The Lion

The lion is a carnivore.
It has a most fur-ocious roar,
Which scares the other beasts, I guess,
Except, perhaps, the lion-ess.

The Manx

Who always yanks   41
The tail off the Manx?

The Leopard

L.

E.

O.

P.

A.

R.

D.

Leopard l e a p e d up in a tree.

D.

R.

A.

P.

O.

E.

L.

On its prey the leopard f e l l.

43

44

The Jaguarundi

The jaguarundi hunts by day
    Then sleeps inside its lair.
And when it wakes it likes to play
    In jaguarundi-wear.

The Black Panther

Black on black
With big eyes green—
At night the panther's sight is keen.
A stalking shadow, sly and sleek,
That every night plays hide-and-seek.

47

The illustrations in this book were done in watercolor on
primed brown paper bags with collage.
The display type was set in Bostonia and Cinderella.
The text type was set in Sabon.
Color separations by Bright Arts Ltd., Hong Kong
Manufactured by South China Printing Company, Ltd., China
This book was printed on totally chlorine-free Enso Stora Matte paper.
Production supervision by Sandra Grebenar and Pascha Gerlinger
Designed by Ivan Holmes and Douglas Florian